The Stone Age

Written by Juliet Kerrigan
Illustrated by Laura Sua

Contents

Collins

Whose hands are these?

Over 25,000 years ago, a group of people put their hands on the walls of a cave and left a mark. Some of them put paint on their hands and pressed them onto the rock. Others put their hands on the cave wall and blew paint through a straw around their fingers.

painted hands

paint was blown
around the hands

This was the Stone Age, but who were these people and
what was it like living 25,000 years ago? No one could
write, but these handprints are the first of many clues
that tell us something about Stone-Age life.

Old, Middle and New

The Stone Age in Europe lasted so long it's been divided into three parts by experts.

Name	Known as	Date
Old Stone Age	the Palaeolithic	800,000 BCE to 10,500 BCE
Middle Stone Age	the Mesolithic	10,500 BCE to 4000 BCE
New Stone Age	the Neolithic	4000 BCE to 2400 BCE

Clues

stone axes,
mammoth bones,
reindeer bones
    and **antlers**

red deer skull "mask"
possibly used on
special occasions

farming tools, pottery

5

Hunting for clues

Like the handprints on the cave walls, there are things that have survived from the Old, Middle and New Stone Age.

Some are easy to find like **monuments** and stone circles.

Some are dug up.

an archaeologist on a dig

Stonehenge was rebuilt several times during the Stone Age.

Some are so large they can only be spotted from the air, using aircraft or **drones**. This track is nearly ten kilometres long, and it may have been used by Stone-Age people for **processions**.

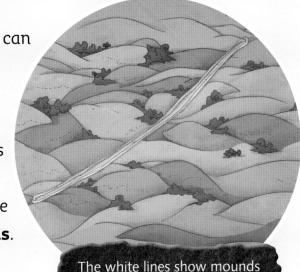

The white lines show mounds of earth either side of the track.

Other clues can only be found with modern technology, using machines that can "see" through earth. Experts using a machine like this discovered about 120 large stones, pushed over and buried under an earth bank.

The stones may have looked like this when they were standing upright.

Tool-makers

There are lots of clues that tell us that Stone-Age man became a tool-maker. Stones and animal bones were made into tools and weapons. They probably used wood too, but **archaeologists** don't often find it because it rots.

sharp end for cutting

an Old Stone-Age hand axe

This hand axe was held here.

Later in the Stone Age, tools like this were fixed into handles made of wood, bone or antler.

The best stone to make a tool or weapon from is called flint. It's very hard and it can be **knapped** into lots of different shapes. Flint was so valuable for making really sharp tools and weapons that Stone-Age people were ready to dig down as deep as 13 metres to find it.

Some stone tools were used for many different tasks, like chopping and pounding. Some were for particular jobs, like scraping animal skins.

Hunting and gathering

At the start of the Stone Age, people didn't stay in one place. They moved about, looking for food such as animals, roots, honey, seeds, nuts and berries. Later, they learnt how to hunt and fish using **harpoon** tips, arrowheads and spear points.

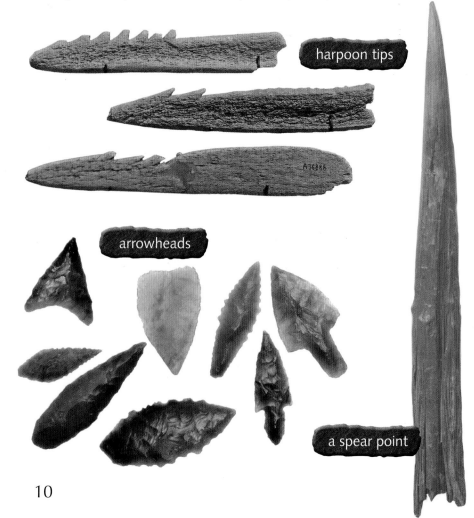

harpoon tips

arrowheads

a spear point

a Stone-Age hunting scene painted on the wall of a cave in Spain

At first, the animals they hunted were mammoth, bison and woolly rhinoceros. As the **climate** got warmer, they hunted for deer and cattle called **aurochs**. Experts have worked out that there was enough meat on one aurochs to feed 100 people.

As they moved around, following the animals, Stone-Age people made campsites.

Farming

Later on in the Stone Age, there were big changes. People were learning how to grow crops like wheat and barley. This meant they didn't move around so much chasing their food.

wool and leather for clothes, shoes and bags

querns

barley

bones for tools

Trees were cut down to make room for fields to grow the crops. Burnt **grain** from the Stone Age has been found, and large stones called querns, for grinding the grain into flour for food.

Animals like cattle and sheep were caught and tamed. These animals could provide meat, milk, wool and leather. Stone-Age people would also have carried on hunting, fishing and looking for fruits and nuts so that they had enough to eat.

meat and milk for food

wheat

13

Clothes

Experts always thought that people in the Stone Age wore furs and animal skins, especially when the weather was very cold. They turned out to be right when the body of a man who died over 5,000 years ago was found frozen in the ice in the mountains of northern Italy.

He was wearing a goatskin coat and leggings fastened to a calfskin belt, a goatskin **loincloth**, a cap made of bearskin and shoes of deerskin and bearskin,

bearskin cap

stuffed with hay in grass netting to keep his feet warm. The clothes had been sewn together with cross-stitch, using bone needles and animal **sinews** for thread.

Later, people learnt how to **spin** and **weave** wool to make into cloth for clothes.

remains of the cape

15

Homes

As more people farmed, they stayed in one place. Instead of camping and moving on, Stone-Age people built houses that lasted longer. Most of these early houses were made of wood, so all that's now left are the holes in the ground where the posts to hold up the roof stood. Some were rectangular and some were round.

This is what the houses may have looked like.

The roofs were covered in **turf**.

People lived in this spot for about 500 years.

The houses were dug into the ground.

There aren't many trees in the Orkney Islands, Scotland, so houses here were made of stone. They had stone **hearths**, stone sleeping platforms and stone cupboards. New Stone-Age people lived here about 3800 BCE.

Handmade

With a more settled life, New Stone-Age people started to make pottery for storing, cooking and serving food. The pots were handmade and often decorated by pressing fingertips, rope or bone combs into the clay. Then they were fired in a bonfire.

When archaeologists find these pots, they're usually in pieces and have to be put together again. One pot found still had hazelnuts and a wooden **stirrer** in it!

This Stone-Age pot has been decorated with lines.

Stone-Age people made things they needed. They also made things for pleasure. A flute made from a bone of a **vulture** shows that people may have enjoyed making music.

It's 40,000 years old!

They also **carved** images on mammoth tusks. This tusk has been carved into the shape of two reindeer, one behind the other.

Tombs and burials

Life was short because of illnesses, injuries and fighting. Many people didn't live beyond the age of 30. Some of the dead were **cremated**, and some were buried.

Over 30,000 years ago, a body was buried in a cave in Wales. The body had been painted with red clay and had a necklace made of seashells. Experts have worked out that it was the skeleton of a young man, and that he ate fish, but no one knows why he was painted red.

Other skeletons have been found in Europe, also covered in red clay. The red paint may have been part of a **ritual**.

This is what the burial might have looked like.

Stone-Age people also buried bodies in stone tombs and then heaped earth over them.

This chamber tomb, made about 5,000 years ago, had lots of human skeletons in it. About 1,000 years later, sea-eagle bones and talons were also put in the tomb.

The tomb is made of piled-up slabs of rock.

Earth is piled on top of the rock.

tomb entrance

Leaving a mark

Despite a harsh and usually short life in the Stone Age, there was still time for other activities.

In Europe, paintings and carvings have been discovered in caves. Most of the paintings are of animals like mammoth, deer, horses and aurochs. There aren't many paintings of human figures.

This open-air carving of a horse and an aurochs was made over 10,000 years ago.

aurochs

horse

This Stone-Age drawing of a mammoth and a wild goat is about 14,000 years old.

The animals may have been painted to teach children how to recognise them, for special gatherings in the caves, or to celebrate a good hunt. Stone-Age people may have believed that, by painting pictures of the animals, they'd be making sure their *next* hunt was successful.

There are also mysterious signs in the caves, like dots and lines, which may never be understood. In some places, animals were carved into rocks in the open air. They may have marked where a certain group of people camped and hunted.

Leaving a mark on the landscape

At the end of the Stone Age, people built tall monuments of earth, wood and stone, which are easy to see, even today. This hill was made of chalk stone, and it was built 5,000 years ago. It's 40 metres high and, if 500 men had worked on it every day, it would have taken ten years to finish. It may have been a special place for Stone-Age people or marked where a certain group of people lived. Today, the hill is covered in grass, but when it was first built, it would have looked white.

Only the postholes remain of wooden monuments.
A reconstruction shows what one of the largest circular
monuments might have looked like when it was
first built.

It may have been used for special meetings, feasts,
ceremonies and hunting games or to mark where
the sun rose or set at certain times of the year.

The nine rings of wooden posts were 100 metres across.

Stone-Age footprints

5,000 years ago, a group of people walked along a salt marsh, among the reeds. Their footprints dried in the sun, were covered by sand and later sealed over by mud. Experts say the prints date from between 5400 BCE and 2300 BCE, but the footprints look as though they were made yesterday.

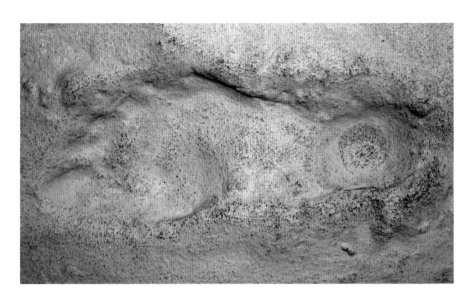

The people who made the footprints lived near the end of the Stone Age. There was still plenty of good flint, but a new way of making tools from **bronze** had arrived. A bronze axe wasn't much sharper than a flint one, but the owner of a bronze axe would seem more important and powerful. Times were changing.

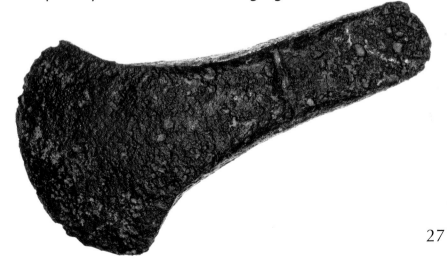

Glossary

antler   bony growth on a deer's head

archaeologists   people who study the past using objects that have been dug up

aurochs   ancient wild cattle, no longer in existence

bronze   metal made from melting tin and copper together

carved   shaped by cutting

climate   weather over a long time

cremated   burnt

drones   aircraft without pilots, controlled remotely

grain   seeds from plants like barley

harpoon   weapon like a spear with a pointed head

hearths   areas in front of fires

knapped   shaped stones like flint by using other stones

loincloth   Stone-Age underwear

monuments   long-lasting special structures or buildings

processions   groups of people moving forward in an organised way

ritual   set way of doing things in a ceremony

sinews   strong, stringy parts of an animal, linking muscles to bones

spin   make fluffy wool into a long thread

stirrer   a stick that works like a spoon

turf   thick mat of grass or other plants

vulture   a large bird of prey that feeds on dead animals

weave   make threads into cloth

Index

Stone-Age life

Old Stone Age

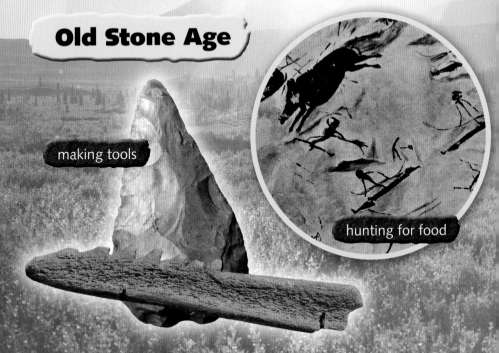

making tools

hunting for food

Middle Stone Age

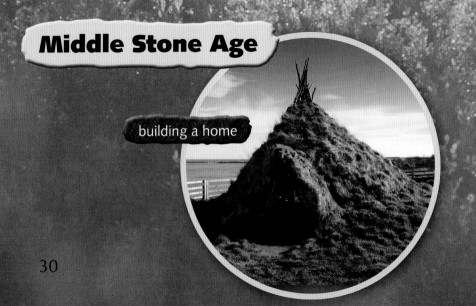

building a home

New Stone Age

farming the land

building big

burying the dead

making pottery

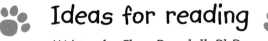

Ideas for reading

Written by Clare Dowdall, PhD
Lecturer and Primary Literacy Consultant

Reading objectives:
- retrieve and record information from non-fiction
- ask questions to improve understanding
- draw inferences and justify these with evidence
- make predictions from details stated and applied

Spoken language objectives:
- articulate and justify answers, arguments and opinions
- use spoken language to develop understanding through speculating, hypothesising, imagining and exploring ideas

Curriculum Links: History - changes in Britain from the Stone Age to the Iron Age

Resources: modelling clay, ICT, paint for print making

Build a context for reading

- Ask children to share anything that they know about the Stone Age. Help children understand when the Stone Age was by making connections with other known historical times.
- Look at the front and back covers of the book and create a "what we know" list based on evidence and ideas. Ask if anyone has visited Stone-Age ruins, e.g. Stonehenge.
- Read the blurb. Ask children to suggest what life would have been like in the Stone Age (prompt for ideas about food, clothing, shelter).

Understand and apply reading strategies

- Read the contents and discuss what sort of information the book contains.
- Raise questions that the group would like to explore through reading.